AF228951

EXPLORING GREEK MYTHOLOGY

Don Nardo

San Diego, CA

© 2025 ReferencePoint Press, Inc.
Printed in the United States

For more information, contact:
ReferencePoint Press, Inc.
PO Box 27779
San Diego, CA 92198
www.ReferencePointPress.com

LIBRARY OF CONGRESS CATALOGING-IN-PUBLICATION DATA

Names: Nardo, Don, 1947- author.
Title: Exploring Greek mythology / by Don Nardo.
Description: San Diego, CA : ReferencePoint Press, Inc., [2025] | Includes
  bibliographical references.
Identifiers: LCCN 2023047236 (print) | LCCN 2023047237 (ebook) | ISBN
  9781678207809 (library binding) | ISBN 9781678207816 (ebook)
Subjects: LCSH: Mythology, Greek--Juvenile literature.
Classification: LCC BL783 .N3445 2025 (print) | LCC BL783 (ebook) | DDC
  292.1/3--dc23/eng/20240125
LC record available at https://lccn.loc.gov/2023047236
LC ebook record available at https://lccn.loc.gov/2023047237

CONTENTS

Tales from the Mists of Time

Murmurs of awe and excitement rippled through the massive crowd. Athens's entire population had formed an enormous ring around the city's rocky central hill—the Acropolis. Gazing upward, they could see two giant figures standing at the summit, each several times the height of a human and thereby towering over the nearby temples and other buildings. The male, holding his famous three-pronged spear—or trident— was Poseidon, lord of the seas and brother of the chief god, Zeus. The female figure, decked out in gleaming battle armor and carrying an array of weapons, was Poseidon's niece, Athena, Zeus's daughter and goddess of war and wisdom.

All the onlookers knew why the two deities had graced the city with their presence. Word had spread the day before that Zeus had called for his daughter and brother to take part in a contest. At that moment in time, Athens had no patron deity, or special divine protector, and the winner of the contest would earn that coveted role. The rules stated that each competitor needed to strive to create something extraordinarily useful for the city. Zeus himself would decide the winner.

The crowd quickly fell silent as Poseidon strode across the hilltop, his expression indicating he was looking for a spot to his liking. Finding it near the Acropolis's eastern edge, he deliberately jammed his mighty trident into the ground, and a huge geyser-like spray of water burst from that spot. Impressed, the members of the crowd applauded and cheered.

Then it was Athena's turn. She also carefully inspected the hill's summit until finding what she deemed the appropriate spot and quietly pointed an index finger at it. At first, nothing happened, and muddled whispers spread through the crowd below. Almost an entire minute went by, and finally a small green plant stem grew upward from a small patch of soil. Swiftly, it sprouted branches and leaves, and within another few minutes it had become a full-size tree. To be more exact, it was Greece's first olive tree.

This time the applause from the audience was thunderous. The people readily realized that groves of such trees would provide the city with foodstuffs and economic wealth for centuries to come. And resplendent Zeus apparently agreed, for he wasted no time in choosing his daughter as the contest's victor. She thereafter served as Athens's patron deity, and the residents proudly nicknamed her Athena Polias, or "Athena of the City."

Crucial Elements of Classical Greek Society

In the 500s BCE—a great many centuries after that colorful contest atop the Acropolis had supposedly taken place—Athens flourished at the height of what modern historians call Greece's Classic Age (ca. 500–323 BCE). It was the glorious era in which the Greeks invented democracy, embraced the formal study of science, and founded the Western theater tradition. In those same years they also erected the majestic Parthenon temple and hundreds of other splendid stone monuments and defeated the Persian Empire (then the strongest realm on earth). Simultaneously, three Athenians—Socrates, Plato, and Aristotle—gave the Western world the discipline of philosophy.

One thing the Greeks of that eventful epoch did not invent or introduce was the great corpus, or collection, of myths, of which the story of the first olive tree was but one. Those wondrous tales had come from the mists of time. They had originated, the classical Greeks believed, in a remote past era and had been passed down from one generation to another.

To the Greeks of Socrates's time, those inherited stories served several vital functions. The old myths established the origins of the gods that the Athenians and other Greeks devoutly worshipped. Moreover, many of those tales described events that people assumed had actually occurred, which made the myths in a loose sense historical documents. Finally, many myths were morality tales that defined right and wrong and justice versus injustice, and that made them critical components of the education of each new generation of Greeks. And like the tale of Athena and Poseidon, these tales were also entertaining and easily remembered.

Trying to Date the Heroic Age

However, the Greeks were never able to ascertain one important attribute of the myths—namely, where these remarkable stories had originated. To their credit, the thinkers and scholars of the Classic Age attempted to solve that mystery. As an educated guess, they concluded that the people depicted in the myths and their achievements had been quite real but that those events had happened long, long ago. It was thought that in that extremely remote time, magical events abounded, bigger-than-life heroes challenged and overcame evil, and the gods walked the earth and interacted with humans. The Greeks of Socrates's era called that fantastical primeval period the Age of Heroes.

Although it was accepted by almost all the classical Greeks, this theory was based on conjecture. No one could say with certainty how long in the past the supposed heroic age had existed. Was it ten generations? Twenty or thirty? Even more? There was simply no way to be sure.

In marked contrast, modern scholars possess a much clearer vision of the progression and events of ancient Greek history. This is because they have a host of scientific tools that the ancients lacked, especially the discipline of archaeology, the study of past civilizations. During the past two centuries, archaeologists have been able to date Greece's heroic period to roughly a thousand years before Socrates's time. Those experts say that the Age of Heroes probably coincided with the latter part of Greece's Bronze Age, in which people made their tools and weapons from bronze, an alloy of copper and tin.

Reality Morphs into the Magical

What the classical Greeks did not know, and modern historians do, is that during the late Bronze Age, Greece was occupied by a surprisingly advanced earlier civilization. It featured two separate proto-Greek peoples. On the islands of the Aegean Sea dwelled the Minoans, who erected huge, ornate palaces and conducted vigorous trade across the eastern Mediterranean sphere. Greece's mainland, meanwhile, was the home of Mycenaeans, who spoke an early form of Greek. They also built palaces and massive stone walls to protect them.

Archaeological evidence indicates that the prosperous Minoan-Mycenaean civilization rapidly declined and collapsed between 1200 and 1100 BCE. The reasons remain unclear and are still debated by scholars. More importantly, the people of the region descended into a cultural dark age in which the palaces were abandoned; the arts, literacy, and recordkeeping largely disappeared; life overall became village centered; and poverty was the rule.

Ancient Greece (Circa 500 BCE)
BLACK SEA
Thrace
Macedonia
Troy
AEGEAN SEA
Mt. Olympus
Thessaly
Persian Empire
Lesbos
Thermopylae
Delphi
Chios
Thebes
Attica
Corinth
Marathon
Olympia
Mycenae
Ithaca
Athens
Argos
Peloponnesus
Delos
Naxos
Megara
Sparta
N
Rhodes
Crete
MEDITERRANEAN SEA

Furthermore, and crucially, says University of Louisville historian Robert B. Kebric, over time most memories of the vanished society faded, and in general, people forgot their own heritage. Recollections of key leaders and events gave way to "a tangled collection of orally transmitted stories that had been corrupted [and] embellished over the centuries." These tales often mixed with fables that had been simply made up, and the world described in those stories morphed into a magical past that had never actually existed. That distant age, Kebric adds, became as far removed to the classical Greeks "as the Columbus story is to us today."[1]

This romanticized mythical world was, not surprisingly, compelling to the classical Greeks. They "cherished legends of that resplendent past," the late, great scholar C.M. Bowra wrote. Those later Greeks saw in that "lost society something heroic and superhuman, which embodied an ideal of what men should be and do and suffer. Their imaginations, inflamed by ancient stories of vast undertakings and incomparable heroes, of gods walking on the earth as friends of men [formed] a vision of a heroic world which they cherished as one of their most precious possessions."[2]

CHAPTER ONE

The Rise of the Olympian Gods

The minor nature goddess, or nymph, Adrastia stealthily made her way along a path that wound up one side of Mount Aegaeon in the wilds of the large Greek island of Crete. She had to be careful that no one saw her. This was because Gaia, the great divine spirit inhabiting the planet itself, had assigned her a vital and very secret task. A few months before, Gaia had approached Adrastia and another nymph, Ida. Their mission was to covertly guard and raise a young male god who would be in danger if found by his father.

Obediently, the two nymphs set up a small, comfortable household in a cave inside Mount Aegaeon and left its confines only to fetch milk and food for the child. According to an ancient hymn from the region, the boy slept "in a cradle of gold," and for milk "sucked the rich nipple of the she-goat Amalthea." For food the infant consumed "the sweet honeycomb"[3] of local Cretan bees. And over time the child grew into a boy.

One day, carrying a basket filled with several honeycombs, Adrastia entered the cave and found Ida conversing with the young god, whose name was Zeus. He was excited because his mother, a goddess named Rhea, was scheduled to pay him one of her yearly visits. Sure enough, Rhea appeared less than an hour later. Now that he was six and almost an adult (since gods matured far faster than humans did), she told him, it was finally time to reveal to him his origins and heritage.

Rhea began the story by telling Zeus that he was a member of the divine race known as the Titans. Moreover, he was the sixth and last child sired by her husband—Cronos, leader of those gods. The other five children were Hera, Hades, Hestia, Poseidon, and Demeter, Rhea added. Worried that his offspring might rebel against him, the mean-spirited Cronos had swallowed the first five babies directly after their births. (They remained alive in his gut, since as gods they were immortal.) Rhea wanted to put a stop to this disturbing behavior, so when she gave birth to Zeus, she fooled her husband by wrapping a stone in a blanket and claiming it was the new infant. The dim-witted Cronos swallowed the stone, and Rhea secretly entrusted baby Zeus to her mother, Gaia, who in turn asked Adrastia and Ida to secretly protect and raise the child.

Hearing this singular tale, Zeus was both sad and angry. He told his mother and the two nymphs that he felt compelled to become a champion of justice and free his imprisoned siblings from Cronos's bloated belly. To that end, he bade the three goddesses a temporary farewell, left the cave, and headed toward a confrontation that would forever alter history. Although he did not foresee it at that moment, soon he would lead a new race of gods in a universe very different from the one into which he was born.

Nurturing a Respect for the Gods

This well-known myth about Zeus's secret upbringing was one of several stories about the gods that every classical Greek learned as a child. In the same manner that young Christians learn about Jesus's childhood and the stories of his ministry and subsequent

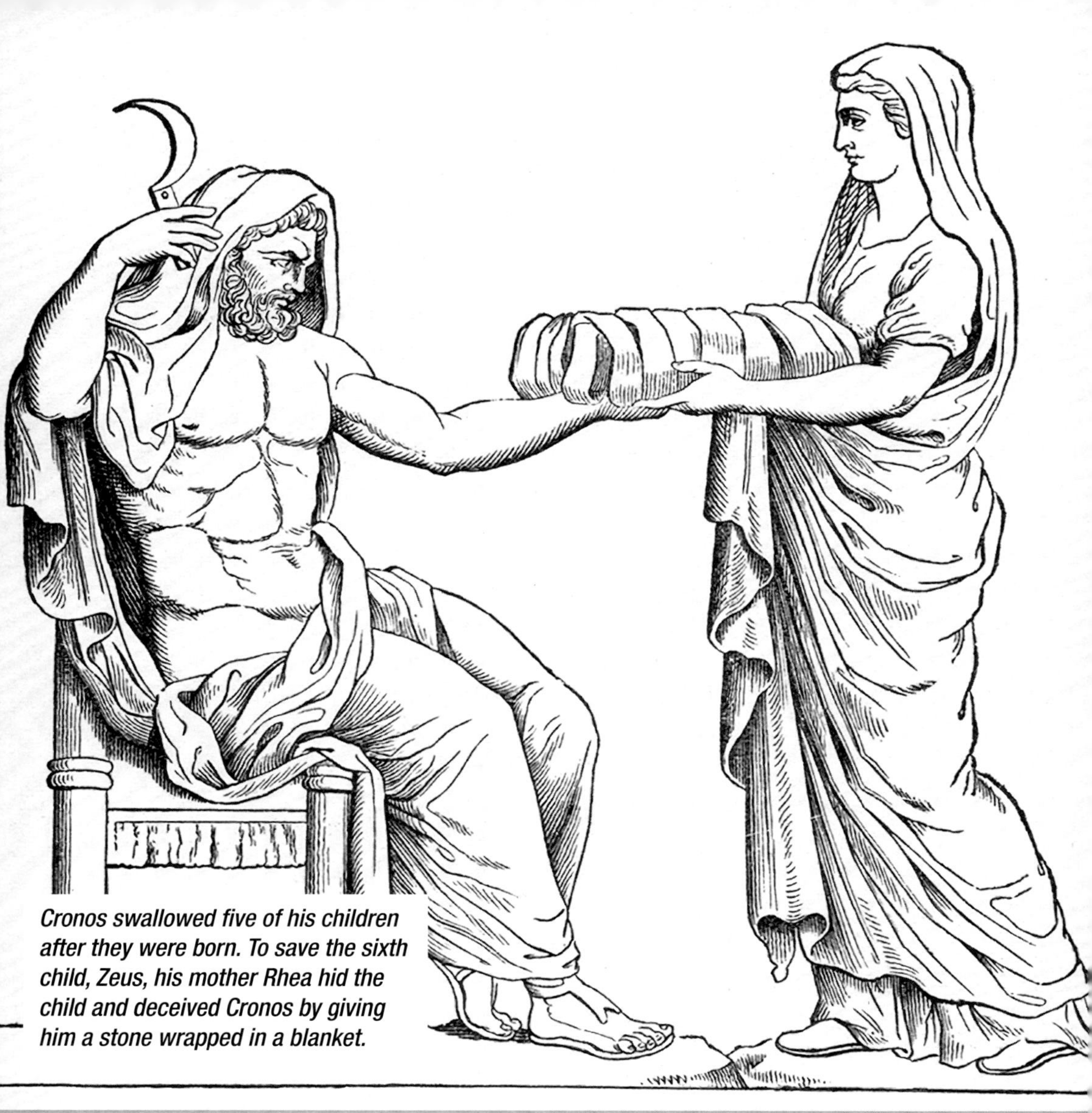

Cronos swallowed five of his children after they were born. To save the sixth child, Zeus, his mother Rhea hid the child and deceived Cronos by giving him a stone wrapped in a blanket.

death and resurrection, young Greeks absorbed the dozens of tales that told how the gods they worshipped—Zeus and his Olympians—came to be.

The ancient Greeks did not view these myths about the gods the way people do today. To modern eyes, these tales are quaint folklore that almost everyone finds colorful and entertaining. The ancient Greeks agreed that those stories were entertaining, but they were also the cherished foundation of their religion. Most classical Greeks were devoutly religious, and their everyday lives were mightily influenced by their beliefs in the gods. In the words of the fourth-century-BCE Athenian scholar Plato, "All men who have any degree of right feeling, at the beginning of every enterprise, whether great or small, pray to the gods."[4] Indeed, births, marriages, funerals, meals, public meetings, and even battles were always accompanied by some form of religious ceremony.

In classical Greece, showing such respect to the gods was vital to the welfare of each community. It was thought that pleasing a deity made it more likely that the god would shower good fortune on a city and its people. The idea that the gods acted and behaved like people reflected how the Greeks viewed these beings. It was assumed the gods had humanlike bodies, personalities, and emotions. Therefore, those deities must feel anger, joy, pity, fear, and sorrow, as well as make mistakes they later regret, just as people do.

Nevertheless, two major factors made Zeus and the other divine beings quite distinct from humans. First, the gods were immortal, while humans grew old and died. Also, the divinities possessed immense power, including the ability to control the weather. Comparing humans to the gods, the fifth-century-BCE Greek poet Pindar said, "From a single mother we both draw breath. But a difference in power in everything keeps us apart."[5]

Freeing His Swallowed Siblings

That enormous power wielded by Zeus and the other gods is no better illustrated than in the tumultuous events that transpired after he left the nymphs' cave and set out to save his brothers and sisters. First he visited another nymph he knew and from her acquired a small bag containing a powdered form of a potent drug. His plan was to secretly sprinkle it in Cronos's food and thereby get him to vomit up the now fully grown gods languishing within him.

During his journey to mainland Greece, Zeus thought about the other things his mother had divulged to him. She had told him how his grandmother, Gaia, had long ago mated with Uranus, the god who personified the overhead dome of the sky. At first they had produced only monstrous offspring, including homely one-eyed giants called Cyclopes. But eventually Gaia and Uranus produced a race of physically beautiful divine beings—the Titans. Besides Cronos and Rhea, among the others were Oceanus, lord of the seas; Phoebe, goddess of prophecy; Hyperion, the sun deity; Iapetus, god of death; and Prometheus, a wise being who could foresee certain future events.

Zeus asked himself why only a handful of these kin criticized Cronos for swallowing his own children. But that was an issue for later, the young deity realized. At the moment, his focus was on drugging his disgraceful father, which, after reaching the val-

This painting shows Cronos abducting one of his children before swallowing it. Zeus later rescued all five of his siblings, whom Cronos had swallowed, by drugging Cronos, which caused him to vomit up the children, now grown into adults.

The Greek Myths in Modern Culture

Without the influence of the Greek myths, the arts and literature of Western civilization would have been very different. The characters and stories of the Greek myths, including those about the rise of the Olympian gods, survived the collapse of the ancient world. These mythical elements came to constitute a substantial portion of the arts, literature, and other creative aspects of Western civilization. "Even the briefest survey of the modern uses of those ancient tales," historians Mark P.O. Morford and Robert J. Lenardon point out, "cannot help but forcibly remind us [of] the potent inspiration that mythology provides for all facets of creative artistic expression." The late historian Michael Grant agreed. He added that "without these myths, we would be hard put to understand the arts and literature and ways of thinking of the West" during the centuries that elapsed "since the [ancient] world came to an end." Repeatedly, Grant concludes, "these products of ancient imagination have been used to inspire fresh creative efforts, which amount to a substantial part of our whole cultural inheritance."

Mark P.O. Morford and Robert J. Lenardon, *Classical Mythology*. New York: Oxford University Press, 2010, p. 491.

Michael Grant, *Myths of the Greeks and Romans*. New York: Plume, 1995, p. xvii.

ley where Cronos dwelled, Zeus managed to do. It did not take long for the king of the Titans to turn green and begin upchucking the beings he had long ago gobbled down. To Zeus's relief, one after another, out came Poseidon, Hera, Demeter, Hades, and Hestia.

The five rescued deities were happy to meet their brother Zeus. However, all six siblings were shocked and disturbed that so few Titans had openly condemned their leader. Together, Zeus and his siblings decided that they must overthrow Cronos and take charge of the Titans, even if it meant going to war with them.

The Titanomachy

As it turned out, Cronos himself sought such a war to put his rebellious children in their place. As the two sides prepared for battle, Zeus plotted to strengthen his ranks, in part by persuading some of the Titans to join him. Among them were Prometheus and his brother Epimetheus and their mother, Themis. Prometheus later related why he sided with Zeus:

> I knew the appointed course of things to come. My mother had many times foretold to me that not brute strength, not violence, but instead cunning must give victory to the rulers of the future. This I explained to [Cronus and his supporters], which they found not worth one moment's heed. Then, of the courses open to me, it seemed best to take my stand—my mother with me—at the side of Zeus.[6]

As Zeus's forces continued to grow, Cronos began to worry. He hurried to gather his own followers and to warn them that they must capture and imprison Zeus and his five siblings. Otherwise, the Titans might lose their place as masters of the universe.

Finally, both sides were ready, and the fatal conflict—which the classical Greeks called the Titanomachy, or "War of the Titans"—commenced. Day after day, year after year, the combatants raged against one another with all their strength. Some uprooted large trees and used them as clubs. Others grasped enormous boulders and hurled them miles into the air.

The unremitting fighting dragged on and on with neither side obtaining a strategic advantage. Then the shrewd Prometheus, still fighting for Zeus, realized that no one had thought to exploit a potentially huge military asset. He told Zeus that the giant Cyclopes that Gaia had birthed long before were trapped far underground in a gloomy region called Tartarus. Uranus had imprisoned them there, along with more of his and Gaia's monstrous progeny—including ones that had one hundred hands. Those fearsome creatures hated Cronos, Prometheus pointed out, so Zeus should free them and enlist them to help fight the Titans.

Zeus happily took this advice and scurried down into the shadowy depths. Reaching the massive stone doors leading into Tartarus, he hurled a thunderbolt, which shattered the lock, giving him access. He then released the three largest Cyclopes—Thunderer, Lightener, and Shiner—who quickly began forging new weapons for him. Zeus also freed the "Hundred-Handers," as they were called, each of which could simultaneously throw one hundred spears or rocks.

A New Race of Gods

With these formidable allies, Zeus was able to bring the long, destructive war to its gargantuan climax. "The boundless sea rang terribly around and the Earth crashed loudly," wrote the seventh-century-BCE Greek poet Hesiod. "Wide heaven was shaken and groaned, and high [Mount] Olympus reeled from its foundation under the charge of the undying gods, and a heavy quaking

Zeus throws lightning bolts as he fights along with his allies to drive Cronos and the Titans from Olympus.

reached dim Tartarus. . . . The cry of both armies as they shouted reached to starry heaven."[7]

During this furious fighting, Hesiod went on, Zeus demonstrated why he deserved to be the universe's overseer. In a terrifying charge, he dashed down from the heavens, tossing glowing shards of lightning as he went. "The bolts flew thick and fast, [and] the life-giving Earth crashed around [and] the vast forests crackled loud with fire all about."[8]

Soon the exhausted Titans had had enough and surrendered. According to Hesiod, the victors imprisoned their defeated enemies in Tartarus's "everlasting shade." Furthermore, Zeus gave orders that "they may never leave," and to make sure of that, three of the Hundred-Handers readily agreed to forever patrol that region's borders "as faithful guards."[9]

After their momentous victory, Zeus and his followers took charge of the world and began rebuilding those parts that had sustained horrendous damage during the conflict. They erected magnificent new palaces atop towering Mount Olympus, inspiring the famous nickname for themselves—the Olympians. Also, their

Did the Gods Actually Live atop Mount Olympus?

Today people who write about ancient Greek civilization at its height during the Classic Age (500–323 BCE) often say that the Greeks of that era envisioned their gods dwelling atop Mount Olympus. This is a mistaken notion, however. Modern historians have concluded that the idea of Olympus being the home of the gods had developed many centuries earlier, during the cultural dark age (ca. 1150–850 BCE) that followed the collapse of Greece's Bronze Age society. Over time this concept persisted, but it steadily came to be seen as only a quaint fable. And by the start of the Classic Age, few if any Greeks believed such a thing was real or even possible (in part because many people had by then climbed Mount Olympus and had found no trace of divine beings). Instead, the common wisdom had become that the gods lived in some unknown quarter of the sky. Moreover, some classical Greek thinkers came to suggest that the gods might not exist at all. For instance, the Epicureans, followers of Epicurus (ca. 341–270 BCE), preached that even if those deities did exist, they likely lived far from Earth and paid no attention at all to humans and their petty problems.

roles and duties were now formally confirmed. Zeus's brother Poseidon was god of the seas; their sister Hera, whom Zeus married, was protector of women. Demeter was goddess of plants, Hestia oversaw hearths, and Hades took charge of the underworld. Later added to the Olympian ranks were other immortals, including Zeus's daughter Athena, the goddess of war and wisdom; his son Apollo, the master of prophecy; and Hephaestus, blacksmith to the gods.

Thus, a new race of deities rose to power to control the universe. No humans yet existed. But after their creation, they—the earliest Greeks—would come to respect and worship those deities for their unsurpassed power. What is more, the Greeks would be endlessly enthralled by the beauty of those beings. As the late, great mythologist Edith Hamilton wrote, unlike the formless or monstrous gods feared by members of many ancient faiths, "the world of Greek mythology was not a place of terror for the human spirit." With very few exceptions, the Greek Olympians "were entrancingly beautiful with a human beauty, and nothing humanly beautiful is really terrifying. The early Greek mythologists transformed a world full of fear into a world full of beauty."[10]

CHAPTER TWO

Myths of the Homeric Epics

Achilles was the prince of Phthia, a kingdom in central Greece. He was known as the finest fighter in the Greek-speaking lands. One day he opened a dispatch a messenger had handed him. The letter was from Menelaus, king of the Greek realm of Sparta. The Spartan ruler was furious, he wrote, because Paris, prince of the independent trading city of Troy, had run off with the Spartan queen, Helen. To retrieve her and punish Paris, Menelaus was calling for as many Greek kings and princes as possible to join in an expedition against Troy. A great many of those rulers had already accepted, the letter's author added.

Achilles wanted to join the great military undertaking, but when he mentioned it to his mother, the sea goddess Thetis, she grew angry and forbade it. Her reason was that many years before, she had heard a divine prophecy that predicted if there was ever a conflict between the Greeks and Trojans, her son would die in it. In fact, to help protect him, when he was an infant she had dipped his body into the Styx, the river that formed the border of the dark and scary underworld. It was said that human skin exposed to that murky liquid would thereafter be resistant to injury. In the words of the late historian W.H.D. Rouse, Thetis "dipped him in the awful river of Styx, to make his body safe against wounds, but she had to hold him by the heel and ankle, and so his heel was left unprotected."[11]

Worried for her son's very life if he joined the expedition, Thetis secretly took him to the house of Achilles's wealthy uncle. There the uncle promised he would do everything he could to hide the young man. As part of the ruse, Achilles wore women's clothes day and night to ensure that no one recognized him.

There was one individual in Greece astute enough to see through all this trickery, however. Desperate to find Achilles, Menelaus turned to Odysseus, king of the Greek island kingdom of Ithaca, who was known for his cleverness. After tracking Achilles to the uncle's mansion, Odysseus pretended to be a traveling salesman of women's finery. For the women of the household, he laid out some makeup, perfumes, ribbons, and other items, but he also mixed in a sturdy new sword.

Odysseus saw that most of the women eagerly began examining the makeup and perfumes. However, one of them ignored those items and picked up the sword, swinging it back and forth with the expertise of a warrior. Achilles thereby revealed himself to Odysseus, who took him aside. The Ithacan king chided his friend for resorting to deception to avoid the coming war, and after tendering an apology, Achilles agreed to bring a contingent of his own soldiers to Troy.

Little did either man realize the consequences of joining the expedition. Achilles would end up dying within Troy's towering walls, thereby fulfilling the prophecy his mother had heard. And Odysseus was fated to be kept away from his throne and family for twenty danger-filled years, ten at war and ten trying to get home.

Foundational Texts in Western Literature

It is fitting that Achilles and Odysseus interacted this way on the eve of the expedition to Troy. Each of those men became the protagonist, or main character, in one of the two greatest epic poems

ever composed in ancient times—the *Iliad* and the *Odyssey*. These are the earliest surviving examples of Western literature and to this day are seen as among the finest.

These marvelous stories, each made up of dozens of separate myths, were neither created by one person nor penned all at once in their present highly complex form. Historians think that much shorter and more rudimentary versions of them appeared sometime in the tenth or ninth century BCE. At first the two tales passed from one generation to another strictly in oral form; that is, traveling bards, or storytellers, publicly recited them from memory, and each bard added a few new details or improved existing lines and phrases. In this manner, the epics grew longer and more polished over time.

Of those storytellers, the last and almost certainly the most talented to leave his mark on the two epics was Homer. His are the versions that the Greeks fi-

ODYSSEUS

King of the Greek island of Ithaca, he led a contingent of ships and men to Troy. At war's end, he and his men wandered for ten years on the journey homeward.

nally wrote down sometime in the 600s BCE. Committing them to writing in a sense froze or crystalized them in the magnificent form that every subsequent generation has inherited and enjoyed.

The Finest Warrior Refuses to Fight

In a very real sense, the two Homeric epics together form one long story. First comes the *Iliad*. It begins in the last year of the Greeks' ten-year siege of Troy, an ancient city in the northwestern sector of what is now Turkey. After Achilles, Odysseus, Menelaus, and the other Greek aristocrats had arrived at Troy with their combined army, nine grueling years of war had elapsed. Neither side had been able to score a knockout blow to the other.

That standoff was fated to change in the conflict's tenth year. First, Achilles had a falling-out with Agamemnon, Menelaus's brother and leader of the expedition. They argued over their claim to a beautiful female slave taken as a prize during the conflict. When Agamemnon kept the girl and refused to give her to Achilles, the latter, in a huff, retired to his tent. He and his men would no longer fight before Troy's lofty walls, Achilles announced.

The Greeks' Most Beloved Poet

The birth year of Homer, the ancient Greeks' favorite poet, remains unknown. In fact, no one knows for sure whether he was a real person. Still, most modern scholars accept that Homer existed and that he lived sometime in the 700s BCE, give or take a couple of decades. One of the traveling bards who recited long epic poems, he is credited with producing the final versions of two already existing works. The first, the *Iliad*, describes a series of events near the end of the famous mythical Trojan War; the second epic, the *Odyssey*, recounts the subsequent adventures of Odysseus, one of the several Greek kings who took part in the conflict. Still, historians are unsure whether Homer contributed to both epics. Some experts have suggested that he might have expanded and finalized only one of them. (A few scholars have even proposed that someone else may have finalized both works.) Attempts to resolve these uncertainties about Homer's existence, birth date, and contributions to the epics continue, and the experts routinely refer to the overall debate as the "Homeric question."

This incident seriously altered the balance of power in the war by putting the Greeks at a severe disadvantage. Without Achilles, whose fighting prowess inspired all the Greek soldiers, they began to lose one battle after another. In one of those encounters, the greatest of the Trojan champions, Hector (son of Troy's king), led a contingent of his men in a wild assault that drove the Greeks backward almost to their camp near the beaches. Desperately worried, one of the Greek kings, Nestor of Pylos, shouted to Agamemnon, "Calamity is certainly upon us!"[12]

Achilles's Great Moment of Triumph

Even though it was clear the Greeks were in serious trouble, mighty Achilles still refused to leave his tent and fight. This motivated his best friend, Patroclus, to don Achilles's armor and enter the fray. Seeing that armor and thinking that Achilles had reentered the war, the Trojans grew fearful and retreated toward the city. As the Greeks gave chase, Patroclus and Hector met up on the plain and fought. The Trojan champion easily defeated and killed Patroclus, and when Achilles found out what had happened, he immediately became a changed man. Swearing he would never rest till he had avenged his slain friend, Achilles rejoined the Greek army, which now drove the entire Trojan force back inside the city.

Only one Trojan, valiant Hector, refused to flee. He remained outside the walls, waiting for Achilles to meet him in single combat. Soon the Greek army approached, and from its ranks strode Achilles, who eagerly faced off with his Trojan nemesis. As Homer narrated, "Hector charged, brandishing his sharp sword [and] Achilles sprang to meet him, inflamed with savage passion."[13] Seconds later the two champions crashed together, and loud cheers rang out from the watching armies. The fight that followed was both brutal and exciting. In the end, Achilles saw an opening and thrust his spear into his opponent's neck. "Hector came down

After a brutal and exciting fight, Achilles used his spear to kill Hector.

in the dust," Homer wrote, "and the great Achilles triumphed over him. [The onset of] death cut Hector short and his disembodied soul took wing for the House of Hades [the underworld]."[14]

Achilles's great moment of triumph turned out to be short-lived, however. Soon after Hector's demise, his brother Paris, who was standing atop Troy's battlements, shot a magic arrow. The shaft struck the only vulnerable spot on Achilles's body—his heel—and he fell dead in the dust. Despite the loss of their best warrior, however, it was not long afterward that the Greeks won the war and sacked Troy.

Troubles in Thrinacia

In Homer's *Odyssey*, Odysseus and his men faced some particularly dangerous encounters when they reached the island of Thrinacia (an ancient name for Sicily, off Italy's southwestern coast). First, while traversing the strait separating Thrinacia from Italy, they were attacked by a gigantic sea monster named Scylla. Raising its bulky body high above the ship, it snatched six sailors, dragged them away, and began eating them alive. This provided an opening for the rest of the horrified crewmen to escape. Not long afterward, however, the Greeks were almost pulled to their deaths by an immense whirlpool that the local Italians called Charybdis. Odysseus later recalled that "when she swallowed the salt water down, the whole interior of her vortex was exposed, the rocks re-echoed to her fearful roar, and the dark sands of the sea bottom came into view." After these frightening episodes, Odysseus and his men stopped to rest on Thrinacia, where they slaughtered and ate some local cattle. They had no idea that those beasts belonged to Helios, god of the sun. When he found out, he complained to the chief god, Zeus, who hurled a thunderbolt at the vessel, demolishing it. Only Odysseus survived to continue his journey.

Quoted in Homer, *Odyssey*, trans. E.V. Rieu. Baltimore, MD: Penguin, 1961, p. 195.

From One Dangerous Place to Another

The actual architect of that victory was Odysseus. As Homer mentioned briefly in the *Odyssey*, the Ithacan king came up with the idea of constructing a huge, hollow wooden horse and hiding several soldiers inside. Leaving the massive object near the beach, the other Greeks boarded their ships and sailed away.

The Trojans assumed the enemy had given up the conflict and left the horse as a sacrifice to the war goddess Athena. Some Trojan soldiers dragged the horse into the city, where it became the centerpiece of an enormous victory celebration held that evening. Late that night, however, after everyone was fast asleep, Odysseus and his companions quietly climbed out of the horse and opened the gates for the Greek army that had sailed back under the cover of darkness. The ten-year siege of Troy ended with the city's destruction.

A few days later, Odysseus prepared for his departure with the twelve ships he had brought with him a decade before. He knew that his island kingdom lay less than a week's journey across the Aegean Sea's blue-green waters. And he looked forward to seeing his family again, especially his wife, Penelope, and son, Telemachus, who had been a small child when Odysseus had departed for Troy.

The Ithacan ruler was not destined to enjoy that brief and peaceful trip, however. Soon after Odysseus's vessels headed out to sea, an enormous storm struck, and he and his men became hopelessly lost. For month after month, year after year, they were forced to wander from one strange, often dangerous place to another. In one hair-raising incident, they lost several ships and their crews to a race of huge cannibals. And in a different, equally remote location, a divine sorceress named Circe turned many of the sailors into pigs; fortunately for them, Hermes, patron deity of travelers, forced Circe to change them back.

The Dangerous Journey Home

One of the most frightening incidents during the long journey took place on an uncharted island inhabited by a tribe of the one-eyed giants known as Cyclopes. Odysseus later recalled that these brutal and uncivilized creatures "have no assemblies for the making of laws, nor any settled customs." Instead, they dwell "in hollow caverns in the mountain heights."[15]

When Odysseus took a few men ashore to gather food and water, they became trapped in the cave where a Cyclops named Polyphemus lived with his herd of goats. With a massive boulder blocking the cave entrance, the monster proceeded to kill and eat some of the Greeks. As the appalled Odysseus later told it, "Their brains ran out on the ground and soaked the earth. Limb by limb, he tore them to pieces to make his meal, which he devoured like a mountain lion."[16]

On their long journey home, Odysseus and his men became trapped in the cave of the Cyclops Polyphemus. Although some men were eaten, the remaining men eventually tricked Polyphemus and escaped.

Eventually, the surviving men devised a plan to escape. After Polyphemus fell asleep, they sharpened a wooden pole and drove it through the giant's eye, blinding him. That allowed them to slip by him unseen when Polyphemus, sightless but still following his daily routines, pulled back the boulder to let his goats out to graze.

In the years that followed, more dangerous and lethal situations led to the loss of all of Odysseus's ships and men. And after a full decade of wandering—his second since leaving for Troy—he alone managed to make it back to Ithaca. There, he found that his beloved wife, Penelope, was being plagued by a group of well-to-do suitors, who, assuming he was long since dead, demanded that she marry one of them. In addition, they had permanently taken over the palace's banquet hall and regularly helped themselves to the estate's food, wine, and other amenities.

Offended and angry, Odysseus decided that the suitors must die. While devising a plan to make that happen, he disguised himself as an old beggar. One exception he made was to reveal himself to and reunite with his now grown son, Telemachus. When the timing was right, they trapped the suitors in the banquet hall and slew them one by one.

Thereafter, Odysseus was finally reunited with Penelope. The two were so joyful that they wished their initial embrace might go on and on. From afar, the goddess Athena heard that wish and with a wave of her hand prolonged the lovers' touching moment by delaying the coming of the dawn. It warmed the deity's heart that this stalwart and noble soldier's unrelenting search for home had ended at last.

CHAPTER THREE

Villainous Tales

Zeus, leader of the Greek gods, had many love affairs, some with goddesses, others with human women. Out of all these relationships, the one he regretted the most was a romance with a lovely ocean nymph named Plouto. For Zeus, the problem was not Plouto herself; rather, it was the mortal son he had sired by her—Tantalus. The latter was destined to become the human most hated by all the gods for eternity.

The saddest part of Tantalus's story, those deities agreed, was that it could well have ended on a happy rather than horrific note. Indeed, when Plouto's son was a youth, the gods absolutely adored him. They frequently invited him to dine with them in their palaces atop lofty Mount Olympus, and sometimes he threw dinner parties for them at his own, humbler abode in southern Greece.

What Zeus and the other divinities did not realize was that Tantalus's friendly demeanor toward them was only an act. For reasons unknown, he secretly envied and despised his father and the other Olympians. So intense was his hatred for them that eventually all he could think about was finding some way to humiliate them. He knew that killing them was out of the question because they were immortal.

Finally, the young man hit upon a plan he believed would thoroughly embarrass the deities. He plotted to secretly transform them into bestial, savage cannibals. To that end, Tantalus murdered his own son, the innocent and kindly Pelops.

Slicing up the boy's corpse, he put the pieces in a big pot of stew, which was slated to be the main course at a supper he had invited the gods to attend.

Tantalus's dastardly scheme largely failed, however, because he did not anticipate just how sensitive the gods' sense of smell was. When a servant placed the bowls of stew before those divine guests, they instantly detected the hideous contents of the food and refrained from eating it. One exception was the goddess of plants, Demeter, who by accident swallowed a small piece of one of Pelops's shoulders.

Seething with fury, the deities decided that death was too lenient a punishment for Tantalus. In the *Odyssey*, Homer recounted the eternal penalty they laid upon him in the underworld:

> [He] was standing in a pool of water which nearly reached his chin, and his thirst drove him to unceasing efforts. But he could never get a drop to drink. For whenever he stooped in his eagerness to lap the water, it disappeared. . . . [Also, luscious fruits dangled] above his head, [but] whenever [he] tried to grasp them . . . the wind would toss them up towards the shadowy clouds.[17]

TANTALUS

A son of Zeus, he was initially loved and respected by the gods, but he secretly harbored a hatred for them. When he turned on the gods, they punished him severely.

For Every Hero a Villain

Tantalus is one of several characters in the Greek myths who is either wicked or the pawn of a greater evil. By virtue of their bigger-than-life exploits, such villains are certainly among the most colorful aspects of those old tales. However, to the ancient Greeks such scoundrels were not simply entertaining, they were also instructional. In Greek eyes, they demonstrated the perils of ignoring or discarding cherished social, political, and moral values.

Moral behavior was extremely important to the Greeks. The villains and their exploits exemplified and reinforced moral themes that ran through the entire corpus of myths. Almost every legendary tale made some sort of statement about good versus evil, and it was expected that good would triumph in the end. Greek thinkers suggested that if villains succeeded in these tales, then the narratives would threaten the cosmic order and perhaps render the gods, who usually stood for justice, purposeless.

Therefore, for every mythical character who did good or heroic deeds, there tended to be a villain who would be defeated and often punished in the end. These evildoers took many forms. Some, like Tantalus, were ordinary people who for one reason or another did dishonest or destructive acts. Other common villains included tyrannical rulers and terrifying monsters. As Edith Hamilton put it, the villains are "present in any number of shapes, [but] they are there only to give the hero his reward of glory. What could a hero do in a world without them?"[18]

Zeus Versus Hideous Typhon

In fact, many Greek mythical heroes received their "rewards of glory" by slaying villains who took the form of frightening monsters. Sometimes these monster slayers were human, and other times they were divine beings. The chief god, Zeus, for example, though sometimes an ethically flawed individual, bravely slew more than his share of monsters.

One of the most hideous and heinous of those evil beasts was Typhon, one of the early monstrous offspring of the earth goddess Gaia. One ancient writer described the creature as "a mixture of man and beast, the largest and strongest of all [Gaia's] children." Typhon was huge and deformed; it had a "hundred heads of serpents . . . [and] all of his body was winged, and the hair that flowed in the wind from his head and cheeks was matted and dirty." In addition, "a great storm of fire boiled forth from his mouth."[19]

Gaia, who seriously disliked Zeus for defeating her other progeny—the Titans—convinced Typhon to battle and hopefully capture and imprison the leading Olympian. But although the monster was physically formidable, the scheme had a major flaw. Namely, like many of the monsters from the Greek myths, Typhon was not very bright. He should have approached Zeus as quietly as possible to effectively ambush him. Instead, the creature noisily lumbered along, and the god felt the vibrations that passed through the ground. That gave Zeus time to prepare several of his emblematic thunderbolts, which could fry the flesh of any living thing.

It was Zeus, then, who ended up ambushing Typhon, and the encounter shook all of Europe to its foundations. One after another, the deity hurled his bolts of lightning, which burned many of the monster's body parts to a crisp. Finally, Typhon became so weakened that Zeus easily tossed him into the deepest pits of the underworld.

A Monster with a Grim Duty

One of the best-known monsters in the corpus of Greek myths is Cerberus, a huge, three-headed, vicious doglike creature. He guarded the borders of the underworld to make sure no human souls who entered that dark realm ever escaped. Cerberus was "a dreaded hound," the Greek epic poet Hesiod said, "who has no pity." For any soul who tried to leave that subterranean kingdom, the great beast "lies in wait for them and eats them up." It was common knowledge that no one was allowed to kill Cerberus. This was because Hades, god of the underworld, had, with the approval of his brother Zeus, given the monster the grim duty it performed. However, Cerberus could be captured, as proved by the famous strongman Heracles (today better known as Hercules). At the request of a curious Greek king, the muscular hero managed to subdue the beast, place it in a cage, and display it to that monarch and his subjects. Heracles was careful, however, to return Cerberus to the underworld right afterward.

Quoted in H.G. Evelyn-White, trans., *Hesiod, The Homeric Hymns, and Homerica*. Cambridge, MA: Harvard University Press, 1964, p. 135.

A Look That Turned People to Stone

Although Typhon is certainly one of the scariest and most destructive villains in the annals of Greek mythology, he is not the most famous. That distinction goes to Medusa, her name derived from a Greek word meaning "queen." With her sisters—Stheno, or "strong," and Euryale, meaning "far jumper"—she was one of the three vicious, evil beings known as the Gorgons.

Dwellers on a remote island, the three frightful sisters had—according to legend—large tusks, serpentine tongues dangling from their mouths, and poisonous snakes for hair. Even worse, when a person or animal gazed upon the meanest and most lethal of the three—Medusa—that individual swiftly turned to stone. This spelled doom for anyone who mistakenly landed on the island.

Eventually, however, Medusa found herself threatened by Perseus, the son of the god Zeus and a mortal woman named Danae. The daring young warrior made it his mission to end the chief Gorgon's reign of terror. From the start, however, Perseus was aware of the difficulties of defeating such a powerful creature as Medusa. He fully realized that he did not know the location of the far-off island where Medusa dwelled. Nor did he know a way to avoid being turned to stone as he approached the monster.

Unsure of how he would face Medusa, Perseus was surprised and felt fortunate when two of the Olympian deities suddenly came to his aid. First, Hermes, messenger of the gods, told him the location of the Gorgons' island; he also gave Perseus a pair of winged sandals that allowed him to fly and a magic hat that made the wearer invisible. The other divinity, Athena, presented Perseus with a polished metal shield in which he would be able to see Medusa's reflection, which did not have the petrifying power of looking directly at her.

Perseus was able to cut off Medusa's head, pictured here, by using Hermes's winged sandals, which allowed him to fly, and a magic hat that made the wearer invisible, enabling him to sneak up on her.

With these boons at his disposal, Perseus flew directly to the island. There, from high above, he witnessed a troubling sight. As the ancient Roman poet Ovid put it, "No matter where he turned he saw both man and beast turned into stone, all creatures who had seen Medusa's face."[20] Minutes later, the young hero caught sight of his prey resting atop a large boulder. Because he was invisible, thanks to Hermes's hat, she was blissfully unaware of his presence. Cautious to look at her only via her reflection in the shield, Perseus dove downward and swung his razor-sharp sword, neatly separating her horrifying head from her equally hideous body.

Evil Woman or Victim?

After Perseus slew Medusa, the Greek-speaking lands were, at least for a few years, safe from being terrorized by monstrous creatures. People were not safe, however, from the harmful acts perpetrated by human villains, who existed in every kingdom and city. Perhaps the most notorious of these ne'er-do-wells was the sorceress Medea. She appears in several myths, beginning with the one in which she first met her future husband, the well-known hero Jason.

Literary and Artistic Works About Medea

The female villain Medea has fascinated people worldwide since her myths first appeared sometime in the early first millennium BCE. And writers and artists of all kinds have portrayed her and her deeds in their works right up to the present day. The first important artistic work about her was the Greek playwright Euripides's classic play, *Medea*, first presented in Athens in 431 BCE. Later, several Roman writers, including Ovid and Seneca, produced plays about Medea. Also, a number of modern writers have penned plays based on Medea's myths. Among the several popular novels about Medea are Dorothy M. Johnson's *Witch Princess* (1967) and H.M. Hoover's *The Dawn Palace* (1988). In addition, more than two dozen composers have produced music based on Medea's exploits; an outstanding example is the ballet *Medea* (1947) by American composer Samuel Barber. Meanwhile, dozens of great modern actresses have played Medea onstage. Seen as iconic in the role was English actress Judith Anderson, who won a Tony Award in 1947 for her portrayal. Later, in 1970 Italian director Pier Paolo Pasolini filmed Euripides's *Medea*, with Maria Callas in the title role. And in the 1963 movie *Jason and the Argonauts*, Nancy Kovak portrayed the character.

This picture shows Jason and Medea stealing the Golden Fleece, with Medea putting its dragon guard to sleep.

Jason and his followers, known as the Argonauts, embarked on a quest to find the Golden Fleece, the hide of a magical ram. To that end, they voyaged to a remote land and stole the fleece from the local king with the aid of his daughter, Medea. Claiming to suddenly be in love with Jason, she betrayed her family and country and escaped with the Argonauts to Greece.

Reaching the kingdom of Iolcos, Jason presented the fleece to the local ruler, Pelias, who had earlier requested that Jason retrieve that object. In exchange, Pelias had promised to give the throne to Jason, but now the king reneged on that vow and refused to step down. In response, Medea bewitched Pelias's daughters into murdering their own father.

The city's people reacted to the murder by driving Medea and Jason away. The two next settled in Corinth (in south-central Greece) and there had two children. At first it seemed as if the family would be happy. But then Jason had a secret love affair with Glauce, daughter of Corinth's king, and agreed to marry her. When Medea found out, first she murdered Glauce and then decided to further punish her unfaithful husband by slaying their children. After that, she mounted a chariot pulled by dragons and raced away in hopes of starting a new life in Athens.

Throughout the ages, most people familiar with Medea's story have seen her as either evil or criminally insane. Yet a few expert observers have proposed that she was, at least regarding her killing of her own children, a victim of Jason's betrayal of her. In her tale, as told by the ancient Greek playwright Euripides, she insists that she is justified in slaying the children and that the gods tolerate that act. Euripides seems to be suggesting that the cosmos is permeated by certain vague, primitive, violent forces and urges that can drive people to do things they would normally deem unthinkable. In the words of the late historian H.D.F. Kitto, Medea might be viewed as the victim of those "blind and irrational forces we can neither understand nor control—only participate in."[21]

The ancient Greeks were as divided about Medea as modern experts are, with some seeing her as a villain and others as a victim. Yet in general, all the Greeks were fascinated with moral concepts, particularly the never-ending struggle between good and evil. And the content of their myths demonstrates this. The villains of these tales were, and remain, key players in the eternal fight between light and darkness.

CHAPTER FOUR

The Triumphs of Heroes

In the distance, the muscular Athenian prince, Theseus, could make out the coastline of the large Aegean island of Crete. In command of a sturdy warship carrying dozens of warriors, he prepared to attack Knossos, capital of the Cretan kingdom ruled by King Minos. That tyrannical monarch had recently kidnapped fourteen Athenian teenagers—seven boys and seven girls. Theseus was determined to get them back, assuming they were still alive.

Thinking back on the events of recent years, Theseus recalled that the ongoing hostage situation was not new. Almost every year for more than a decade, Minos had taken fourteen Athenian boys and girls to intimidate Athens. His goal was to keep that kingdom within his large sphere of political and economic influence. At first, Theseus's father, King Aegeus, had felt he lacked the power to resist the Cretan bully. But Theseus had finally persuaded him to at least try, thereby leading to the present expedition against Minos.

When the Athenian vessel reached Crete, Theseus urged his soldiers to hurry, for the hostages, if still alive, were in danger. Not long after bringing each batch of children to Knossos, Minos had locked them in the Labyrinth, a maze of tunnels running beneath his sprawling palace. There, one by one, they were killed and eaten by the Minotaur, a bloodthirsty beast that was half human and half bull.

Both Theseus and Aegeus agreed that battling the creature was highly risky. But Theseus "urged his father to take heart," the ancient Greek biographer Plutarch wrote. The young man assured the king that he would be successful. Just in case, however, Plutarch went on, "Aegeus gave the [ship's] pilot a second sail, a white one, and ordered him on the return voyage to hoist the white canvas if Theseus was safe, but otherwise to sail with the [standard] black sail as a sign of mourning."[22]

Hoping to be able to fly the white sail later, Theseus led his men in their surprise attack on Knossos. Killing the palace

After the tyrannical monarch of Knossos kidnapped fourteen Athenians, Theseus took a warship to get them back. He rescued the Athenians, then slew the infamous Minotaur (pictured).

Heroism of the Highest Order

Greek mythology also celebrates heroic women. One of the best known is Antigone, a daughter of Oedipus, king of Thebes. Her fame rests on her solution to an ethical dilemma that rocked both her family and her country. When her brothers, Polynices and Eteocles, drove their father from the city and seized the throne, Eteocles turned on Polynices. The latter responded by launching an assault on Thebes, and soon afterward the brothers slew each other in single combat. Their uncle, Creon, then assumed power. In a thoughtless move, he proceeded to deny Polynices a decent burial, an act that all Greeks, real and mythical alike, saw as both sacrilegious and criminal. Yet at first no one had the courage to defy this barbaric order, mainly because Creon threatened to kill anyone who did so. Disturbed and disgusted, Antigone decided to risk all by doing the morally right thing. In the light of day, she boldly buried her brother, and the enraged Creon quickly ordered her execution. The Greeks viewed Antigone's courageous action, done despite her knowing she would surely die for it, as an example of heroism of the highest order.

guards, they penetrated the structure, and Theseus alone descended into the massive maze below. By the light of a torch, he found the fourteen hostages still alive and told them to hurry upward and follow his waiting soldiers to the ships. Then he moved further into the maze, where he soon came upon the infamous Minotaur. It appeared surprised to see a strange man in its lair, and before it could react, Theseus thrust the torch into its face, blinding it. Staggering, it fell, after which the hero slew it with his sword.

With the monster dead and the hostages rescued, Theseus and his soldiers sailed back toward Athens. Everyone aboard the ship continued to celebrate as they approached the city, and as a result no one had remembered to take down the black sail and hoist the white one. Seeing the black canvas from the roof of his palace and assuming his son was dead, in a fit of grief King Aegeus jumped to his death. Thereafter, the story goes, to honor that ruler's memory, the Athenians named the waterway bordering Greece's eastern coast the Aegean Sea.

The Spirit of Goodness

It is not surprising that Theseus's righteous effort to save his fellow Athenians from captivity and death remained widely popular in every generation of ancient Greeks. Of the numerous colorful and exciting stories in their collection of myths, most compelling for them were those that explored the concept of *kalokagathia*, meaning "goodness." More precisely, this word denoted the expansive kind of goodness that combines bravery, selflessness, and a strong sense of justice.

Greeks blessed with that rare blend of qualities were seen as *aristos*, or "best," in society. The more common name for them was *heroes*. And those, including Theseus, featured in the myths tended to be larger-than-life characters possessed of uncommon valor and fighting skills.

Besides being fun to hear or read about, these mythical heroes also set examples for ordinary Greeks to emulate. True, most Greeks did not expect to slay monsters or depose tyrannical rulers, as their favorite legendary heroes did. But it was not unusual for Greeks of all ages to try, when possible, to be brave, just, and helpful when faced with life's many choices and challenges.

Moreover, because the Greek myths survived the close of the ancient era and are still popular today, their cultural influence, though not as strong as in the past, remains intact. Some people are still inspired by the powerful spirit of *kalokagathia* that pervades those tales and later stories that were modeled on them. "Embodied in these simple stories," scholar Bernard Evslin suggests, ancient Greek belief in the ultimate power of goodness "has branded itself on the human consciousness forever."[23]

A Hero's Campaign to Right Wrongs

Of all the mythical heroes the Greeks admired, certainly none was burned into their collective consciousness more than Heracles, or, as the later Romans called him, Hercules. Widely acknowledged as probably the greatest hero in all of world mythology, he was unbelievably strong, a trait he inherited from his divine father, Zeus. Heracles was also courageous, generous, and morally upright in the extreme. And his sense of goodness and justice led him on a lifelong campaign of fighting monsters, righting wrongs, and aiding people in need. In Edith Hamilton's words, "He considered himself on an equality with the gods—and with some reason. Whenever he fought with anyone, the issue was certain beforehand. He could be overcome only by a supernatural force."[24]

Heracles tested and retested his fighting abilities time after time in his long, illustrious career. One of the earliest such episodes occurred one summer when he was still in his teens. Reports spread far and wide that the residents of the region controlled by Thebes (in south-central Greece) were in danger. A large lion was repeatedly devouring sheep and other farm animals in the area, and parents feared the creature might add small children to its menu. Hearing this, Heracles wasted no time in tracking down the lion. It attacked him, but he stood his ground, wrestled with it, and then broke many of its bones with a mighty bear hug, a move for which he would subsequently become renowned.

Heracles was unbelievably strong. When he was in his twenties, he killed a supernatural lion that was terrorizing the people of Nemea.

Punished for His Disobedience

A gallant sufferer who was popular with the ancient Greeks was Prometheus, the Titan god of forethought and for a long time a close adviser to Zeus. It was Prometheus to whom Zeus assigned the crucial task of creating human beings. After doing so, the Titan came to care deeply for their welfare. Over time he grew concerned about their lack of knowledge of fire, for they nearly froze to death in the winter. The problem was that Zeus had earlier forbidden anyone from giving fire to the humans, which the chief Olympian insisted must be reserved for the gods. Eventually, Prometheus decided he must defy that rule and introduce fire to his creations. When Zeus found out, he was livid. To punish Prometheus for his disobedience, he had him chained to a large rock on a remote mountaintop. Each day a monstrous vulture clawed out and ate the Titan's liver. That organ rapidly grew back overnight, but the next day the creature returned and repeated the process. To the Greeks, Prometheus's endurance of eternal suffering for doing the right thing made him the paragon of goodness and decency.

It turned out that this was not the only marauding lion that Heracles slew. In his twenties he killed a supernatural one that was terrorizing the people of Nemea, in southeastern Greece. It was the first of a series of so-called labors he did at the request of a Greek monarch named Eurystheus. That ruler wanted to eliminate as many evil, murderous beings as possible. Two of the other labors included destroying a herd of nasty human-eating horses and killing a giant boar that gored several people with its enormous tusks.

Still another of Heracles's labors became one of the most famous monster slayings in Greek mythology. In this case the monster was a many-headed reptilian beast, the Hydra. Legends claimed that the creature had one immortal head and perhaps as many as one hundred ordinary ones. Furthermore, if it lost one head two more grew back in its place. As retold by historians Michael Grant and John Hazel, the strongman used a sword to severe most of the heads and a torch to burn the stumps, which kept new heads from growing. Then, "after disposing of the mortal heads, he chopped off the immortal one and buried it under a rock." After that, he sliced open the monster's body, found a sack filled with poison inside, and "kept it by him to poison his arrows."[25]

Perfect Selflessness and Love

Not all the examples of Greek mythical characters of extraordinary decency, integrity, and kindness were male. Among the several female ones was Alcestis, queen of Pherae, a small kingdom in northern Greece. She and her husband, King Admetus, married when they were in their twenties and for several years enjoyed a carefree, happy life.

One day, however, news came that Apollo, god of prophecy, had made a disturbing prediction. Admetus would die within a few months, the deity said. There was only one way this tragic occurrence could be avoided. Apollo foresaw that if someone in the kingdom freely chose to die in the king's place, the still youngish ruler would live well into old age.

Admetus was too decent and fair a person to ask anyone to die for him, and so he bravely accepted his fate. But his wife, Alcestis, decided she would have none of that. She proceeded to shock everyone in the realm by announcing that she would forfeit her own life to save her beloved husband. Although at first Admetus tried to dissuade her from this, she stubbornly refused to budge and valiantly prepared for her coming demise. Reactions from the citizenry—rich and poor alike—echoed that of a government official who stated, "In my belief she is the noblest wife a man ever had [and] her death will make her famous [because] she is by far the noblest woman who ever lived."[26]

A few days later, as the prophesied moment of death approached, the people of Pherae wore black. All felt sad and hopeless, knowing that soon, Thanatos, god of death, would come for their queen and lead her to the gloomy underworld. When his hand touched hers, they realized, her precious life would be over.

When the god of death came to claim Alcestis, Heracles ambushed him and sent him fleeing in embarrassment. This picture shows Heracles leading Alcestis back to her husband, Admetus.

However, unknown even to the gods, fate had decreed a very different destiny for Alcestis. That same day, the famous monster slayer Heracles, a close friend of the king, happened to drop by the local palace. Hearing what was happening, the big-hearted strongman became determined to stop the prophecy's fulfillment. When the black-robed grim reaper, Thanatos, arrived on schedule to claim his prize, Heracles boldly ambushed him. In a fearsome fight that shook the palace's foundations, the barrel-chested hero defeated the death deity, who fled in embarrassment.

Thus, the no-less-heroic Alcestis was reunited with her thankful husband. Pherae's citizens cheered when the king announced that fate "has been kind to me." One of his friends disagreed, however, pointing out that fate had had no choice. When the elusive forces of destiny had witnessed Alcestis's display of perfect selflessness and love, they simply could not allow this truly noble woman to die. "And that is what has happened here today,"[27] the friend concluded.

A Virtuous Figure for the Ages

Although the Greeks respected and marveled at the good deeds and heroism of characters like Theseus, Heracles, and Alcestis, they also recognized the existence of an alternative kind of heroism. It was defined less by deeds and more by the ability to endure tremendous suffering. Typically, persons possessing this sort of heroic spirit did not deserve the punishment they had received, yet they endured it without being defeated and destroyed by it. According to DePaul University scholar David Simpson, such a gallant sufferer is "fully conscious of the essential hopelessness of his plight." Yet instead of giving up, the sufferer persists and treats it as a challenge. That daring defiance makes the person "a superb [symbol] of the spirit of revolt and of the human condition. To rise each day to fight a battle you know you cannot win, and to do this with wit, grace, compassion for others, and even a sense of mission, is to face the absurd in a spirit of true heroism."[28]

SISYPHUS

Ruler of Corinth who angered the gods by playing tricks on them. As a punishment, he had to roll a huge rock up a hill for eternity.

One of the most famous of these valiant victims in Greek mythology was Sisyphus, the first king of the city of Corinth. Over time Zeus heard that this ruler had played multiple tricks on various deities. On one occasion, for instance, the clever Sisyphus duped the lord of the underworld, Hades, into letting him return to the land of the living.

Exasperated, Zeus inflicted a penalty on Sisyphus that far exceeded the seriousness of his offense. The man had to push a huge boulder up a steep hill; as soon as he reached the top, the rock rolled back down, and the strenuous task had to be endlessly repeated. The classical Greeks, who were intimately familiar with this tale, almost unanimously agreed that in this case Zeus had gone too far. And in so doing, he allowed Sisyphus to demonstrate a heroic spirit that Zeus himself only sometimes displayed. In this way Sisyphus became—like Alcestis and other heroes before him—a virtuous figure for the ages.

CHAPTER FIVE

Stories Explaining the Natural World

Apollo, who was known chiefly as the god of prophecy, had many other functions and duties. He was also a deity of healing, poetry, music, dance, and archery. His love of sporting events sometimes led him to engage in small-scale competitions with other gods or even humans.

Among the few chosen mortals whom Apollo competed with over the centuries, his favorite by far was a young man named Hyacinthus, who hailed from the Greek kingdom of Sparta. The pair held one-on-one contests not only in archery but also in javelin and discus throwing. And as time went on, they became fast friends, even though one was mortal and the other divine.

One day the two entered an open meadow, and Apollo challenged Hyacinthus to still another discus-throwing contest. The boy politely let the god have the first throw. And when the object hurtled upward, the Roman writer Ovid said, it "scattered the clouds in its path and then, after a long time, it fell back again to its natural element, the earth. . . . Immediately, the young Spartan, in his eagerness for the game, ran forward without stopping to think, in a hurry to pick up the discus. But it bounced back off the hard ground, and rose into the air, striking him full in the face. The god grew as pale as the boy himself."[29]

The horrified god hurried to the young man and attempted to halt the bleeding. Normally, this would have taken little effort for a deity with the potent healing abilities that Apollo possessed. But now and then there were cases in which fate, a force stronger than even the gods, interceded and imposed its mysterious will. And the distraught Apollo sensed that this was happening before his tear-filled eyes. Sure enough, mere minutes later, death claimed Hyacinthus's unlucky soul.

According to Ovid, the grieving Apollo cried out, "I wish that I might give my life in exchange for yours . . . or die along with you! But since I am bound by the laws of fate, that cannot be." Nevertheless, he added, the memory of their friendship would be with him always, and he would ensure that the young man's name would never be forgotten. The god proclaimed, "You will be changed into a new kind of flower."[30] And sure enough, the boy's remains were transformed into the first hyacinth, which thereafter grew in abundance across Greece.

How Did Nature's Wonders Come to Be?

Hyacinthus's tragic tale is not the only Greek myth that sought to explain the ancestries of specific flowers that grace the natural world. Another involves Narcissus, a handsome youth who badly treated a young woman who fell in love with him. To teach him a lesson, Nemesis, goddess of revenge, caused Narcissus to fall madly in love with himself. Day after day he did nothing else but stare at his own reflection until he died, and then his body transformed into a new kind of flower—the daffodil (sometimes called the narcissus flower).

Moreover, flowers are but one element of nature whose origin the Greek myths tried to explain. For example, similar stories addressed how the moon, planets, and stars came to be; how lightning, wind, and other kinds of weather phenomena occur; and the causes of natural disasters like earthquakes and volcanic eruptions. Stanford University scholar Adrienne Mayor attests, "Greek

After Apollo challenged Hyacinth to a discus-throwing contest, the discus bounced and struck Hyacinth in the face. He died quickly afterward.

myth is a complex skein [knotted thread] of tales about the origin of the natural world and the history of its inhabitants."[31] In general, before the rise of Greek science in the 600s and 500s BCE, the Greeks believed that nature's countless elements and wonders were created or controlled by various gods. For instance, people referred to the deities in charge of weather-related phenomena as the *theoi meteoroi*, literally the "weather gods."

Zeus and His Thunderbolts

Of that group of divine beings, the most powerful was still Zeus. In addition to being the overall leader of the gods, he had charge of several important aspects of the weather, including rainstorms, thunder, and lightning. Flashes of the latter, which the Greeks routinely called thunderbolts, are now known to be large discharges of electrical energy. But in ancient Greek eyes those brilliant, fiery flares were manufactured by Zeus. In fact, Greek writers, including the great epic poet Homer, frequently described him as the "lightning maker."

It was unknown to the Greeks exactly how Zeus made his thunderbolts, since that process was never specifically addressed in any of the myths. But the idea that he could do so was seen as an indication of his vast power. Even more awesome, he not only unleashed the thunderbolts during storms but also at times hurled them as weapons.

One of the best-known tales in which Zeus employed these lethal armaments was the one in which he and his fellow gods were threatened by an army of giants. Those creatures had rap-

Nature Goddesses Too Numerous to Count

Of all the nature deities in the great corpus of Greek myths, the minor goddesses known as nymphs were by far the most numerous. In fact, more than one ancient writer claimed they were nearly countless. Typically, all of them were attractive young females. And each nymph, or in many cases each group of them, inhabited and controlled one or another specific aspect of nature. The Oreads, for instance, protected mountains. Similarly, the Epimelides oversaw grassy pastures, the Oceanids populated the seas, the Meliae looked after honeybees, the Haliai occupied coastal caverns, the Anthoussai managed flowers, and the Dryades dwelled in forests. Dozens of myths, most often short but charming, featured individual nymphs. One such story, for example, tells of Tanagra, one of the Naiads, or nymphs who watched over wells and springs. One day, the story goes, she caught the eye of Ares, god of war. The problem was that the messenger god Hermes also fancied her. The two deities had a boxing match to decide which would win her, and Hermes was victorious. He took Tanagra to a town in central Greece, which was later named for her.

idly grown from a rain of blood drops released when the ancient sky god Uranus was badly wounded by his own son, Cronos. Once the giants had reached their full size, the earth goddess Gaia, who disliked Zeus intensely, persuaded them to attack him and the other Olympian deities.

During this immense battle, which the Greeks called the Gigantomachy ("War of the Giants"), one of the giants, Mimas, caught sight of Zeus and decided to try to slay him. But as the fifth-century-BCE Greek playwright Euripides put it, the dim-witted ogre was ignorant of the tremendous power of "the thunderbolt, smoldering and irresistible, which Zeus held ready to hurl." When Mimas, his face contorted with rage, charged at his opponent, the latter let loose his signature weapon. A few seconds later the giant had been reduced to a pile of ashes, having been "charred with the flame of the thunderbolt."[32]

Aeolus and His Bag of Winds

Another natural weather phenomenon addressed in several Greek myths is the wind. There were several minor wind gods, among them Zephyros, who oversaw the west wind; Boreas, the north wind; and Notos, the east

Zeus showed his vast power through his thunderbolts. He unleashed them during storms but also at times hurled them as weapons.

wind. The god of all winds, however, was Aeolus, said to live on a highly unusual island. In Homer's epic poem the *Odyssey*, the hero Odysseus remarks that Aeolus's island "floats in the air. It features a very strong bronze wall running around it, with a rocky cliff looming above."[33]

In fact, it is in the *Odyssey* that Aeolus's most famous myth appears. After wandering with his crewmen for a long time through strange seas trying to return to their homeland of Ithaca, Odysseus encountered Aeolus, and the two made a deal. The god would send the west wind, which would carry the ship back home. In exchange, Odysseus later recalled, Aeolus "gave me a bag made of the hide of his own ox and inside he stuffed the winds [except for the westerly one] from all around the area. Aeolus put the bag on my ship and tied it shut with a shiny silver string, making sure that not a single breath of air could escape."[34] The deity made Odysseus agree that the bag would not be opened until the ship made it to Ithaca.

Aeolus then conjured up the west wind, as promised. The voyage was swift and dramatic and the vessel had almost made it home when sudden disaster struck. A few crewmen, thinking the bag might contain treasure, opened it, thereby releasing winds that blew in every direction but westerly. This colossal outburst drove the craft away from Ithaca instead of toward it. Angry about the sailors' tampering with his bag of winds, Aeolus told Odysseus he would no longer offer him any aid and promptly soared away into the sky.

The Most Feared Natural Disasters

Aeolus was a god the Greeks knew not to trifle with because he could conjure up destructive storms. But the most feared natural disasters were earthquakes and volcanic eruptions, which popular myths linked to several different gods and other supernatural beings. It was long believed that Poseidon was among them. Although he was the chief sea god, he also supposedly caused some of the earthquakes that rocked the Greek lands from time to time.

For instance, one myth claimed that in the distant past, some prisoners escaped from their Spartan captors. The runaways took refuge in the local temple honoring Poseidon and were given sanctuary there. But the rulers ordered soldiers to drag the men out and punish them harshly. Enraged at this violation of religious custom, the god unleashed an earthquake that leveled the entire town.

However, not all earthquakes were caused by Poseidon; for example, some were attributed to Enceladus, one of the giants who attacked the gods during the Gigantomachy. According to one tale, during the fight the war goddess Athena lifted up the island of Sicily and dropped it on top of him, trapping him. After that, over the course of centuries he sometimes tried to escape—always unsuccessfully— triggering earthquakes in the process.

Other myths about Enceladus credited him with causing Sicily's volcano, Mount Etna, to erupt. It was said that the fumes and smoke expelled during such eruptions were bursts of the

Hephaestus was the god of forges. Some stories say he had a vast underground workshop equipped with many huge bellows.

giant's hot, foul breath. The third-century-CE Greek writer Philostratus the Elder wrote, "From beneath the earth [Enceladus] renews the fight and breathes forth this [volcanic] fire as he utters threats."[35]

In contrast, most volcanic eruptions in other areas were thought to be caused by Hephaestus, the god of forges. Some old tales say he had a vast underground workshop equipped with many huge bellows. When all of them were in use simultaneously, the story goes, huge amounts of fire and smoke were produced and blasted their way out of the vents of volcanoes.

Enduring Appeal to Human Hearts

In similar fashion, the Greek myths provided explanations for many other aspects of nature, including the objects seen in the day and night skies. The sun, for example, was the gleaming chariot of

Helios, god of the sun. Every day he rode the chariot across the sky, tracing the path from sunup to sundown. Likewise, his sister, Selene, piloted her own chariot, embodying the moon, across the night sky.

Such notions seemed to explain most, though not all, phenomena associated with the sun and moon. Lunar eclipses, for instance, in which much of the moon's disk darkens, required explaining. Accordingly, a myth developed that claimed that now and then human witches used magic to pull Selene and her chariot downward toward earth. In response, the goddess strenuously resisted, and soon the moon regained its normal appearance.

Meanwhile, the stars were seen as small holes in the inner surface of a vast dome that encompassed the sky. Beyond the dome, it was thought, was a region filled with highly intense fire. Ancient Greeks believed that small portions of this heavenly fire were visible through tiny holes in the sky dome, thus producing the stars.

These and other myths about the weather, heavenly bodies, and various aspects of nature were vital for the early Greeks and other ancient peoples. Before the rise of science, factual explanations for such phenomena did not yet exist. And the myths gave people comfort by filling that knowledge vacuum and at least providing them with the illusion that they knew how the world worked.

Perhaps the most remarkable development associated with the Greeks' nature-related tales, and indeed all their myths, was the amazing enduring quality of those stories. Even after modern science eventually explained most of nature's workings, the Greek myths did not fade into obscurity; rather, they survived and thrived. In large part this is because they appeal so much to human minds and hearts. Those tales entertain us and simultaneously remind us about both our virtues and faults. The myths "cover virtually all human experiences," scholar Philip Mayerson points out, including "love, hate, war, tyranny, treachery, courage, [and] fate." In this way, they "provide an endless source of inspiration for the creative imagination."[36]

SOURCE NOTES

Introduction: Tales from the Mists of Time

1. Robert B. Kebric, *Greek People*. Boston, MA: McGraw-Hill, 2005, p. 8.
2. C.M. Bowra, *The Greek Experience*. New York: Barnes & Noble, 1996, p. 32.

Chapter One: The Rise of the Olympian Gods

3. Quoted in Theoi Greek Mythology, "Callimachus Hymns 1–3." www.theoi.com.
4. Quoted in Benjamin Jowett, trans., *The Dialogues of Plato*. Chicago, IL: Encyclopedia Britannica, 1952, p. 447.
5. Quoted in C.M. Bowra, trans., *Pindar: The Odes*. New York: Penguin, 1969, p. 206.
6. Quoted in Philip Vellacott, trans., *Aeschylus: Prometheus Bound, The Suppliants, Seven Against Thebes, The Persians*. Baltimore, MD: Penguin, 1961, p. 27.
7. Quoted in H.G. Evelyn-White, trans., *Hesiod, The Homeric Hymns, and Homerica*. Cambridge, MA: Harvard University Press, 1964, pp. 129, 131.
8. Quoted in Evelyn-White, *Hesiod, The Homeric Hymns, and Homerica*, p. 131.
9. Quoted in Evelyn-White, *Hesiod, The Homeric Hymns, and Homerica*, pp. 46–47.
10. Edith Hamilton, *Mythology: Timeless Tales of Gods and Heroes*. New York: Grand Central, 1999, p. 18.

Chapter Two: Myths of the Homeric Epics

11. W.H.D. Rouse, *Gods, Heroes and Men of Ancient Greece*. New York: New American Library, 2001, p. 134.
12. Quoted in Homer, *Iliad*, trans. E.V. Rieu. Baltimore, MD: Penguin, 1989, p. 258.
13. Homer, *Iliad*, p. 405.
14. Homer, *Iliad*, pp. 405–6.

15. Quoted in Homer, *Odyssey*, trans. E.V. Rieu. Baltimore, MD: Penguin, 2003, p. 142.
16. Quoted in Homer, *Odyssey*, p. 147.

Chapter Three: Villainous Tales

17. Homer, *Odyssey*, p. 187.
18. Hamilton, *Mythology*, p. 19.
19. Quoted in Theoi Greek Mythology, "Typhoeus 1." www.theoi.com.
20. Ovid, *Metamorphoses*, trans. Rolfe Humphries. Bloomington: Indiana University Press, 1967, p. 134.
21. H.D.F. Kitto, *Greek Tragedy*. London: Routledge, 2002, pp. 201–2.

Chapter Four: The Triumphs of Heroes

22. Quoted in Ian Scott-Kilvert, trans., *The Rise and Fall of Athens: Nine Greek Lives by Plutarch*. New York: Penguin, 1984, p. 24.
23. Bernard Evslin, *Heroes, Gods and Monsters of the Greek Myths*. New York: Laurel Leaf, 1984, p. x.
24. Hamilton, *Mythology*, p. 160.
25. Michael Grant and John Hazel, *Who's Who in Classical Mythology*. London: Routledge, 2004, p. 163.
26. Quoted in Philip Vellacott, trans., *Euripides: Alcestis, Hippolytus, Iphigenia in Tauris*. Baltimore, MD: Penguin, 1968, p. 124.
27. Quoted in Vellacott, *Euripides*, p. 157.
28. David Simpson, "Albert Camus," Internet Encyclopedia of Philosophy. www.iep.utm.edu.

Chapter Five: Stories Explaining the Natural World

29. Ovid, *Metamorphoses*, trans. Mary M. Innes. London: Penguin, 2006, p. 229.
30. Quoted in Ovid, *Metamorphoses*, p. 230.
31. Adrienne Mayor, *The First Fossil Hunters: Paleontology in Greek and Roman Times*. Princeton, NJ: Princeton University Press, 2000, p. 193.
32. Quoted in Philip Vellacott, trans., *Euripides: The Bacchae and Other Plays*. Baltimore, MD: Penguin, 1954, p. 41.
33. Quoted in Homer, *Odyssey*, Book 10, lines 4–5, trans. Don Nardo.
34. Quoted in Homer, *Odyssey*, Book 10, lines 6–26, trans. Don Nardo.
35. Quoted in Theoi Greek Mythology, "Enkelados." www.theoi.com.
36. Philip Mayerson, *Classical Mythology in Literature, Art, and Music*. Newburyport, MA: Pullins, 2001, p. 2.

FOR FURTHER RESEARCH

Books

Kenny Curtis and Jillian Hughes, *Greeking Out: Epic Retellings of Classic Greek Myths*. Washington, DC: National Geographic, 2023.

Bernard Evslin, *Bernard Evslin's Greek Mythology*. Los Angeles: Graymalkin, 2023.

Edith Hamilton, *Mythology: Timeless Tales of Gods and Heroes*. 75th anniversary illustrated edition. New York: Black Dog and Leventhal, 2017.

Homer, *The Iliad and the Odyssey*, trans. Samuel Butler. Braga, Portugal: Kathartika, 2021.

Xander Liosis, *Greek Mythology: A Stunning Journey Through Ages and Timeless Stories*. London: Inkwell House, 2023.

Clara MacCarald, *Monsters and Creatures of World Mythology*. San Diego, CA: Brightpoint, 2023.

Lucas Russo, *Uncovering Greek Mythology: A Beginner's Guide into the World of Greek Gods and Goddesses*. Self-published, 2020.

Internet Sources

Mike Belmont, "Poseidon: Greek God of the Sea," Gods and Monsters. www.gods-and-monsters.com.

Celeste, "10 Stories from Greek Mythology That Kids Will Love," *Family Experiences* (blog), January 6, 2021. https://familyexperiencesblog.com.

Ducksters, "Apollo." www.ducksters.com.

Ducksters, "Monsters and Creatures of Greek Mythology." www.ducksters.com.

Alexander Gale, "5 Love Stories from Greek Mythology," Greek Reporter, February 14, 2023. https://greekreporter.com.

Greeka, "Jason and the Argonauts," 2023. www.greeka.com.

Greeking.me, "Ancient Greek Mythology: Olympian Gods, Tales & Daily Life Facts," July 6, 2022. https://greeking.me.

Hellenic Times, "Beasts of Greek Mythology." www.thehellenictimes .com.

Charlotte Higgins, "Fruits of the Loom: Why Greek Myths Are Relevant for All Time," *The Guardian* (Manchester, UK), September 3, 2021. www.theguardian.com.

History.com Editors, "Greek Mythology," History.com, August 27, 2023. www.history.com.

Meghan Mathis, "10 Greek Myths Every Student Should Know," We Are Teachers, October 19, 2021. www.weareteachers.com.

Ohio State University, "Greek Mythology." https://greekarchaeology .osu.edu.

Jana L. Smit, "41 Greek Gods and Goddesses: Family Tree and Fun Facts," History Cooperative, March 31, 2020. https://historycoopera tive.org.

Organizations and Websites

Encyclopedia of Greek Mythology
www.mythweb.com/encyc
This website provides a lot of useful information about both major and minor Greek mythological characters.

Greek Mythology Link
www.maicar.com/GML/index.html
This detailed site has a biographical dictionary with more than six thousand entries and some forty-five hundred photos, drawings, and other images.

Theoi Greek Mythology
www.theoi.com
This is the most comprehensive and reliable general website about Greek mythology on the internet. It features hundreds of separate pages filled with detailed, accurate information, as well as numerous primary sources and reproductions of ancient paintings and mosaics.

INDEX

PICTURE CREDITS

ABOUT THE AUTHOR

Classical historian and award-winning author Don Nardo has written numerous acclaimed volumes about ancient civilizations and peoples. They include more than fifty overviews of the mythologies of the Sumerians, Babylonians, Egyptians, Greeks, Romans, Persians, Celts, Chinese, Hindus, Native Americans, and others. Nardo, who also composes and arranges orchestral music, lives with his wife, Christine, in Massachusetts.